t. Childers

PRAYING WITH
THE EARTH

PRAYING WITH THE EARTH

A Prayerbook for Peace

JOHN PHILIP NEWELL

CANTERBURY
PRESS
Norwich

PICTURE CREDITS

Matzah from *The Golden Haggadah*. The British Library.
The Lindisfarne Gospels. St Mark's Gospel, fol. 94b. The British Library.
Mamluk carpet in the collection of Nasser D Khalili Collection of Islamic Art.
Illustrated in *Treasures of Islam*. Duncan Baird Publishers.
Mosaic tiles from the Alhambra Palace. Illustrated in *Alhambra*.
Frances Lincoln Publishers.

Passages from the Quran are from N.J. Dawood, *The Koran*, Penguin Classics, 1990.

First published in 2011 by the Canterbury Press Norwich
Editorial office
13–17 Long Lane,
London, EC1A 9PN, UK

Canterbury Press is an imprint of
Hymns Ancient and Modern Ltd (a registered charity)
St Mary's Works, 13A Hellesdon Park Road,
Norwich, NR6 5DR, UK

www.scm-canterburypress.co.uk

British Library Cataloguing in Publication data

A catalogue record for this book is available
from the British Library

ISBN 978-1-84825-049-9

Designed and typeset by Vera Brice

Printed and bound by
L.E.G.O. spa–Vicenza, Italy

To Nahum and Rahmah

my Jewish brother and Muslim sister

whose teachings feed my soul

and whose souls feed my longing for peace

THE BLESSINGS OF JESUS

Blessed are those who know their need
for theirs is the grace of heaven.

Blessed are those who weep
for their tears will be wiped away.

Blessed are the humble
for they are close to the sacred earth.

Blessed are those who hunger for earth's oneness
for they will be satisfied.

Blessed are the forgiving
for they are free.

Blessed are the clear in heart
for they see the Living Presence.

Blessed are the peacemakers
for they are born of God.

(The Casa del Sol Blessings of Jesus – based on Matthew 5.3–9)

CONTENTS

PREFACE

This is a time to pray for peace. And it is especially a time to pray for peace within the household of Abraham and Sarah and Hagar. As Jews, Christians and Muslims we are painfully divided, even though we share a spiritual descent. And our divisions are at the centre of much of the world's most serious places of conflict and war today. *Praying with the Earth: A Prayerbook for Peace* is an attempt to utter the longings for peace that are closer to the heart of the household, and closer to the heart of all earth's spiritual traditions, than our divisions.

In the summer of 2008 my wife and I taught a spirituality course on peacemaking at Casa del Sol in the high desert of New Mexico with a Jew and a Muslim. Nahum Ward-Lev, a rabbi from Santa Fe, and Rahmah Lutz, a Sufi Muslim teacher from Abiquiu, reflected with us each day on themes of peace from our distinctive traditions. The pattern was to move into a half hour of meditative prayer after each teaching session.

On one of the days, we used Christian Scripture for our meditation, and I noticed Rahmah's face at the end of the silence. Her countenance was radiant, even more than usual. And when we began to share, Rahmah said: 'I so love Jesus, peace be upon him. He is so compassionate. He is so humble. He is so merciful. I so love Jesus, peace be upon him.' I sat with wonder and tears in my eyes as I listened. And I realised that Rahmah was teaching me how to speak about Jesus, with reverence and with love.

When we open our hearts to one another and share the rich perspectives of our distinct traditions, it is not simply new or foreign insights that we exchange. Sometimes it is ancient and intimate insights that we uncover for one another in the other's tradition. In other words, we need each other if we are to be well. We will be whole not in separation but in relationship. This means that for me as a Christian there are truths about what it means to follow Jesus that I will receive most fully only through other parts of the household.

This is the twofold aim of *Praying with the Earth*, to learn from the wisdom of other parts of the family, and to recover, or perhaps to hear for the first time, some of the lost wisdom in our own branch of the family. And in all of this to be called back to the deep yearnings for peace that are at the heart of our shared inheritance and at the heart of the human soul.

The format of this book is to allow ourselves each day in the morning and evening, at the rising of the sun and at its setting, to listen to the wisdom of our inherited scriptures and to pray, especially for peace. Prayer, or poetry of the soul as I understand it, is about giving expression to the deepest longings of our being. And our deepest longings are for oneness. We come from the One, even though we refer to the Living Presence by different names. We are made of the One. Deep within us, therefore, is the sacred desire for oneness, even though we may live at such tragic distances from it much of the time. The prayers of this book are poetry from the human soul. They may have come through me but they issue from a place deep within us all that longs for peace.

The artwork woven through the prayers and readings of *Praying with the Earth* is from the Hebrew, Christian, and Islamic worlds of art. An appendix at the end of the book indicates which pieces of art have been used and the shared themes that emerge from these distinct spiritual traditions.

Each morning and evening of prayer begins with one of Jesus' blessings or beatitudes as they are usually called in the Christian tradition. These are the words we use every day at the setting of the sun at Casa del Sol, the little spirituality centre in New Mexico that is committed to peacemaking or to what our vision statement calls 'the oneness of the human soul'. The blessings of Jesus call us back to who it is that will show us the way, 'those who know their need', 'those who weep', 'the humble', 'the forgiving', 'those who hunger for earth's oneness', 'the clear in heart', and 'the peacemakers'. They call us back to the people whose hearts yearn for peace. And as Christians they call us back to the heart of the teachings of Jesus, peace be upon him.

My gratitude is to the many people who have touched my life with passionate vision for peace. Their fire lives in my heart and words. Thanks to Sid and Beth Wells who allowed me to hide away in their attic overlooking Galveston Bay, and to Margaret and Van Joffrion in Blowing Rock who provided the same in their Blue Ridge mountain hideout. Solitude during days of writing, plus food and fine company in the evenings, was a priceless gift to this project. Thanks also to Vera Brice for her gifted graphics artistry, and to Christine Smith for her fidelity and vision of publishing. And deepest thanks to the wise editorship of my Ali, without whom I could not imagine writing.

JOHN   PHILIP NEWELL

SUNDAY MORNING

Blessed are those who know their need
for theirs is the grace of heaven.

(Matthew 5.3)

PRAYER OF AWARENESS

Light within all light
Soul behind all souls
at the breaking of dawn
at the coming of day
we wait and watch.
Your Light within the morning light
Your Soul within the human soul
Your Presence beckoning to us from the heart of life.
In the dawning of this day
let us know fresh shinings in our soul.
In the growing colours of new beginning all around us
let us know the first lights of our heart.
Great Star of the morning
Inner Flame of the universe
let us be a colour in this new dawning.

Be still and aware

SCRIPTURE AND MEDITATION

God is our refuge and strength,
a very present help in trouble.

(Psalm 46.1)

Pause

Ask and it will be given you.
Seek and you will find.
Knock and the door will be opened to you.

(Matthew 7.7)

Pause

For every soul there is a guardian watching it.

(Quran – The Nightly Visitant 86.4)

Silence

PRAYER FOR THE LIFE OF THE WORLD

For the gift of this new day
for waking again from the dreams of the night
for our bodies strengthened and our minds renewed
thanks be to you, O God.
You are the stillness of the night
You are the genesis of the morning
You are the moistness of new conception.
Let there be peace in the human soul
let there be wakings to new consciousness
let there be tears of love.
In the life of the world this day
and in our own hearts
let there be fresh tears of love.

Silent prayers for peace

PRAYER OF BLESSING

May the angels of light
glisten for us this day.
May the sparks of God's beauty
dance in the eyes of those we love.
May the universe
be on fire with Presence for us this day.
May the new sun's rising
grace us with gratitude.
Let earth's greenness shine
and its waters breathe with Spirit.
Let heaven's winds stir the soil of our soul
and fresh awakenings rise within us.
May the mighty angels of light
glisten in all things this day.
May they summon us to reverence,
may they call us to life.

SUNDAY EVENING

Blessed are those who know their need
for theirs is the grace of heaven.
(Matthew 5.3)

PRAYER OF AWARENESS

As light gives way to darkness
and the busyness of day concedes to night's stillness.
As conscious thought surrenders to dreams
and our bodies long for rest
we pause to listen
for the beat of your Presence in all things
pulsing in the light of distant galaxies
sounding in the depths of our soul
vibrating in each vein of earth's body.
One Sound as vast as the universe
one universe filled with Presence
one Life within every life.
In the darkness of night
in the stillness that surrounds us
in the unknown depths of our being
we pause to listen.

Be still and aware

SCRIPTURE AND MEDITATION

The compassion of God is for all that has been made.
(Psalm 145.9)

Pause

Come to me, you who are weary and carrying heavy burdens,
and I will give you rest.
(Matthew 11.28)

Pause

By the light of day and by the dark of night
your God has not forgotten you.
(Quran – Daylight 93.1–3)

Silence

PRAYER FOR THE LIFE OF THE WORLD

In lives where love has been born this day
thanks be to you, O God.
In families where forgiveness has been strong
thanks be to you.
In nations where wrongs have been addressed
where tenderness has been cherished
and where visions for earth's oneness have been served
thanks be to you.
May those who are weary find rest this night.
May those who carry great burdens for their people find strength.
May the midwives of new beginnings in our world find hope.
And may the least among us find greatness
strength in our souls
worth in our words
love in our living.

Silent prayers for peace

PRAYER OF BLESSING

In sleep may we be made new this night.
In sleep may we let go of today
and release the worries of tomorrow.
In sleep may we know you
as Soul within our soul
as Guide within our dreams
as Lover within our longings.
In sleep may we be one with you
one with earth's darkness
one with heaven's shining
one with each creature dying
one with each newborn breath.
In sleep may we be one with you
and one with all.

MONDAY MORNING

Blessed are those who weep
for their tears will be wiped away.

(Matthew 5.4)

PRAYER OF AWARENESS

Light
golden light
fresh from the source.
Colours
creation's colours
calling our senses.
Life
life in its oneness
life in its manifold oneness
all from You.
You are the Sun from whom the morning shines
You are the River in whom each life-form flows
each face
each race
each cell within our ever-living soul.
This new day we greet You.

Be still and aware

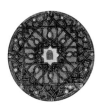

SCRIPTURE AND MEDITATION

Wait for God.
Be strong and let your heart take courage.
(Psalm 27.14)

Pause

Where your treasure is there your heart will be also.
(Matthew 6.21)

Pause

Remember God deep in your soul with humility
and reverence.
(Quran – The Heights 7.205)

Silence

PRAYER FOR THE LIFE OF THE WORLD

For the freshness of this new day
thanks be to you, O God.
For morning's gift of clarity
its light like the first day's dawn
thanks be to you.
In this newborn light
let us see afresh.
In this gateway onto what has never been before
let our soul breathe hope
for the earth
for the creatures
for the human family.
Let our soul breathe hope.

Silent prayers for peace

PRAYER OF BLESSING

On this day
the blessings of heaven.
On this day
the blessings of earth.
On this day
the blessings of sea and of sky.
To open us to life
to ground us in life
to fill us with life
and with wonder.
On those we love this day
and on every human family
the blessings of heaven
the blessings of earth
the blessings of sea and of sky.

MONDAY EVENING

Blessed are those who weep
for their tears will be wiped away.
(Matthew 5.4)

PRAYER OF AWARENESS

At the setting of the sun
in the darkness of the night
with the whiteness of the moon in its splendour
we move with the earth as it turns
we are carried by the hours in their passing
we enter the dark with our years
to seek shelter in night's sanctuary
to find strength for our souls
to know peace in our prayers and our resting.
At the setting of the sun
in the darkness of the night
with the whiteness of the moon in its splendour
we seek peace.

Be still and aware

SCRIPTURE AND MEDITATION

God heals the brokenhearted
and binds up their wounds.
(Psalm 147.3)

Pause

Do not be afraid. I am with you always.
(Matthew 28.10, 20)

Pause

In the remembrance of God our hearts are comforted.
(Quran – Thunder 13.28)

Silence

PRAYER FOR THE LIFE OF THE WORLD

Our heart is comforted
in its awareness of You
Soul within our soul
Life within all life.
Our heart is comforted
in remembering You
Giver of this day
Gift of every moment.
May we be bearers of comfort.
May we be strong in our soul
to cry at the wrongs of nations
to weep with the bleeding earth
to mourn with those who mourn this night
in the loss of life and lands
in the loss of dreams and hope.
May we be strong in our soul this night.

Silent prayers for peace

PRAYER OF BLESSING

Peace for the earth and its creatures
peace for the world and its peoples
peace for our fathers
peace for our mothers
peace for our brothers and sisters.
The peace of heaven's vastness
the peace of ocean depths
the peace of earth's stillness
to bless us in the night
to bless us this night.

TUESDAY MORNING

Blessed are the humble
for they are close to the sacred earth.
(Matthew 5.5)

PRAYER OF AWARENESS

It is in the depths of life that we find you
at the heart of this moment
at the centre of our soul
deep in the earth and its eternal stirrings.
You are the Ground of all being
the Well-Spring of time
Womb of the earth
the Seed-Force of stars.
And so at the opening of this day
we wait
not for blessings from afar
but for You
the very Soil of our soul
the early Freshness of morning
the first Breath of day.

Be still and aware

SCRIPTURE AND MEDITATION

God lifts up those who are bowed down.

(Psalm 146.8)

Pause

Whoever wishes to be great among you
must be a servant among you.

(Matthew 20.26)

Pause

Why do you not bow to the one whom My own hands
have made?

(Quran – Sad 38.75)

Silence

PRAYER FOR THE LIFE OF THE WORLD

For everything that emerges from the earth
thanks be to you, O God,
Holy Root of being
Sacred Sap that rises
Full-bodied Fragrance of earth's unfolding form.
May we know that we are of You
may we know that we are in You
may we know that we are one with You
together one.
Guide us as nations to what is deepest
open us as peoples to what is first
lead us as a world to what is dearest
that we may know the holiness of wholeness
that we may learn the strength of humility
that together we may live close to the earth
and grow in grounded glory.

Silent prayers for peace

PRAYER OF BLESSING

May the deep blessings of earth be with us.
May the fathomless soundings of seas surge in our soul.
May boundless stretches of the universe echo in our depths
to open us to wonder
to strengthen us for love
to humble us with gratitude
that we may find ourselves in one another
that we may lose ourselves in gladness
that we give ourselves to peace.

TUESDAY EVENING

Blessed are the humble
for they are close to the sacred earth.

(Matthew 5.5)

PRAYER OF AWARENESS

At the ending of the day
in the quiet of the hours
at the interplay of light and dark
we wait with the earth as it rests
that we may give thanks for darkness
that we may open to night's senses
that we may remember the ground from which we come
and know You
as Presence in the mystery
as Evening Breeze in our soul
as Everlasting Strength in earth's body.
At the ending of the day we wait
that we may know You
as Lover of the night
as Lover in the night.

Be still and aware

SCRIPTURE AND MEDITATION

God leads the humble in what is right.

(Psalm 25.9)

Pause

The Son of Humankind came not to be served but to serve.

(Matthew 20.28)

Pause

God has brought you forth from the earth like a plant
and to the earth God will restore you.

(Quran – Noah 71.17–18)

Silence

PRAYER FOR THE LIFE OF THE WORLD

For the sacred earth
its scents and sounds and sights
we give you thanks, O God.
For the holy heavens
their heights and depths and breadth
we give you thanks.
May we love the earth
and cherish her fecundity.
May we love the rivers
and obey their ancient purity.
May we love the skies
and honour their infinity
all for one another.

Silent prayers for peace

PRAYER OF BLESSING

Glory be to you
Great Creating Spirit
who shines in distant stars beyond numbering.
And on earth peace.
Glory be to you
Great Creating Spirit
who sings and wings in birds on high.
And on earth peace.
Glory be to you
Great Creating Spirit
whose thunder shakes the shining firmament.
And on earth peace.
Glory glory glory
and on earth peace.

WEDNESDAY MORNING

Blessed are those who hunger for earth's oneness
for they will be satisfied.

(Matthew 5.6)

PRAYER OF AWARENESS

All things come from you, O God,
and to you we return.
All things emerge in your great river of life
and into you we vanish again.
At the beginning of this day
we wake
not as separate streams
but as countless currents in a single flow
the flow of this day's dawning
the flow of this day's delight
the flow of this day's sorrows
your flow, O God,
in the twistings and turnings of this new day.

Be still and aware

SCRIPTURE AND MEDITATION

Sing to God a new song.
Sing to God, all the earth.

(Psalm 96.1)

Pause

In everything
do to others as you would have them do to you.

(Matthew 7.12)

Pause

Whoever saves a human life
shall be regarded as though they had saved all humankind.

(Quran – The Table 5.32)

Silence

PRAYER FOR THE LIFE OF THE WORLD

All things are born of you, O God.
We carry within us your light and your life.
In the mystery of matter
and deep in the cells of our souls
are your longings for oneness.
The oneness of the universe
vast and vibrating with the sound of its beginning.
The oneness of the earth
greening and teeming as a single body.
The oneness of the human soul
a sacred countenance in infinite form.
Grant us your longings for oneness, O God,
amidst life's glorious multiplicities.

Silent prayers for peace

PRAYER OF BLESSING

Blessings on the day
born of night.
Blessings on the earth
wedded to heaven.
Blessings on the creatures
adored by angels.
Blessings on our bodies
alive with spirit.
Blessings on our minds
filled with dreams.
Blessings on our hearts
opened by love.
Blessings, blessings, blessings.

WEDNESDAY EVENING

Blessed are those who hunger for earth's oneness
for they will be satisfied.

(Matthew 5.6)

PRAYER OF AWARENESS

At the close of day
as busyness fades
as light dims
and footsteps soften
we open again the inner door of our being
to enter stillness
to feel our way through the dark
to You
the Silence from whom we are born
the Name before names were spoken
the Love of life's beginnings.
At the close of day
we come.

Be still and aware

SCRIPTURE AND MEDITATION

May God grant you your heart's desire.

(Psalm 20.4)

Pause

Many will come from east and west
and eat together in the garden of God.

(Matthew 8.11)

Pause

Whichever way you turn there is the face of God.

(Quran – The Cow 2.115)

Silence

PRAYER FOR THE LIFE OF THE WORLD

Whichever way we turn, O God, there is your face
in the light of the moon and patterns of stars
in scarred mountain rifts and ancient groves
in mighty seas and creatures of the deep.
Whichever way we turn, O God, there is your face
in the light of eyes we love
in the salt of tears we have tasted
in weathered countenances east and west
in the soft skin glow of the child everywhere.
Whichever way we turn, O God, there is your face
there is your face
among us.

Silent prayers for peace

PRAYER OF BLESSING

May heaven's guardians of night
welcome us.
May heaven's messengers of grace
bless our dreams.
May heaven's angels of compassion
protect our sleep.
That we may wake
refreshed.
That we may wake
with eyes of wonder.
That we may wake
to the world's oneness.
That we may wake
to serve earth's heaven-blessed oneness.

THURSDAY MORNING

Blessed are the forgiving
for they are free.
(Matthew 5.7)

PRAYER OF AWARENESS

We wake
to the forgiveness of a new day.
We wake
to the freedom to begin again.
We wake
to the mercy of the sun's redeeming light.
Always new
always gift
always blessing.
We wake
to the forgiveness of this new day.

Be still and aware

SCRIPTURE AND MEDITATION

God is merciful and gracious
slow to anger and abounding in steadfast love.
(Psalm 103.8)

Pause

Forgive
not seven times but seventy times seven times.
(Matthew 18.22)

Pause

Return evil with good
and your enemy will become your friend.
(Quran – Revelations Well Expounded 41.34)

Silence

PRAYER FOR THE LIFE OF THE WORLD

May our enemy become our friend, O God,
that we may share earth's goodness.
May our enemy become our friend, O God,
that our children may meet and marry.
May our enemy become our friend, O God,
that we may remember our shared birth in you.
May we grow in grace
may we grow in gratitude
may we grow in wisdom
that our enemy may become our friend.

Silent prayers for peace

PRAYER OF BLESSING

The blessings of sun
the blessings of moon
the blessings of east and of west
to guide us on the way
to lighten our eyes
to strengthen our will and our loving.
The blessings of earth
the blessings of air
the blessings of fire and of water
to fill us with heaven
to free us with mercy
to stir us with flames of compassion.

THURSDAY EVENING

Blessed are the forgiving
for they are free.
(Matthew 5.7)

PRAYER OF AWARENESS

Not because
we have made peace this day.
Not because
we have treated the other as our self.
Not because
we have walked the earth with reverence today
but because there is mercy
because there is grace
because your Spirit has not been taken from us
we come
still thirsting for peace
still longing to love
still hungering for wholeness.

Be still and aware

SCRIPTURE AND MEDITATION

As far as the east is from the west
so far does God remove our sin from us.
(Psalm 103.12)

Pause

Do not judge and you will not be judged.
(Matthew 7.1)

Pause

Do not walk proudly on the earth.
You cannot rival the mountains in stature.
(Quran –The Night Journey 17.37)

Silence

PRAYER FOR THE LIFE OF THE WORLD

The ageless mountains are full of your glory
the vast seas swell with your might
the shining skies expand beyond our imagining
so we pause to praise
we wait in wonder
we listen to learn
of the mountain glory within us
of the sea force in our veins
of love's shining infinity.
Grant us the grace, O God,
to serve this inner universe of soul among us.

Silent prayers for peace

PRAYER OF BLESSING

In the coming hours of darkness
may there be light in our dreams.
In the stillness of sleep
may there be strength for our souls.
In the wakeful watches of night
may there be peace in our minds.
Light for new vision
strength to make sacrifice
peace for our world.
On the pathways of earth's journey this night
let there be peace.

FRIDAY MORNING

Blessed are the clear in heart
for they see the Living Presence.
(Matthew 5.8)

PRAYER OF AWARENESS

At the beginning of the day
we seek your countenance among us, O God,
in the countless forms of creation all around us
in the sun's rising glory
in the face of friend and stranger.
Your Presence within every presence
your Light within all light
your Heart at the heart of this moment.
May the fresh light of morning wash our sight
that we may see your Life
in every life this day.

Be still and aware

SCRIPTURE AND MEDITATION

'Come', my heart says, 'seek God's face.'

(Psalm 27.8)

Pause

Let your light shine before others.

(Matthew 5.16)

Pause

You have but to remember
and you will see the light.

(Quran – The Heights 7.201)

Silence

PRAYER FOR THE LIFE OF THE WORLD

It is when we are still
that we know.
It is when we listen
that we hear.
It is when we remember
that we see your light, O God.
From your Stillness
we come.
With your Sound
all life quivers with being.
From You
the light of this moment shines.
Grant us to remember you at the heart of each moment.
Grant us to remember.

Silent prayers for peace

PRAYER OF BLESSING

Peace where there is war
healing where there is hurt
memory where we have forgotten the other.
Vision where there is violence
light where there is madness
sight where we have blinded each other.
Comfort where there is sorrow
tears where there is hardness
laughter where we have missed life's joy
laughter when we remember the joy.

FRIDAY EVENING

Blessed are the clear in heart
for they see the Living Presence.

(Matthew 5.8)

PRAYER OF AWARENESS

Clear our heart, O God,
that we may see you.
Clear our heart, O God,
that we may truly see ourselves.
Clear our heart, O God,
that we may know the sacredness of this moment
and in every moment
seek you
serve you
strengthen you
as the Living Presence in every presence.
Clear our heart, O God,
that we may see.

Be still and aware

SCRIPTURE AND MEDITATION

Teach me your way, O God,
that I may walk in your truth.

(Psalm 86.11)

Pause

The presence of God is like treasure hidden in a field.

(Matthew 13.44)

Pause

Speak for justice
even if it affects your own family.

(Quran – Cattle 6.152)

Silence

PRAYER FOR THE LIFE OF THE WORLD

Your Presence
like treasure
hidden in a field.
Your Glory
like gold
buried on the pathway of every moment.
Your Wisdom
like the finest oil
waiting to be pressed from the human heart
from every nation
from every people
from every child.
Your Wisdom, O God,
to show us the way.

Silent prayers for peace

PRAYER OF BLESSING

May the mighty angels of Heaven
guard the four corners of earth this night.
May the mighty messengers of Life
hold in balance the sacred elements of the universe.
May the mighty bearers of Presence
safeguard the direction of our hearts this night
that we may sleep in peace
that we may dream of justice
that we may wake to the world's oneness
that we may wake to the world's newborn oneness.

SATURDAY MORNING

Blessed are the peacemakers
for they are born of God.
(Matthew 5.9)

PRAYER OF AWARENESS

The peace of morning's stillness
the peace of new beginnings
the peace of heaven's kiss
to welcome us to this day
to root us in this day
to free us for this day
that we may grow with the greening earth
that we may grow from the ground of glory
that we may grow in grateful wonder
of You
Gracious Giver of this day
Great Giver of this new day.

Be still and aware

SCRIPTURE AND MEDITATION

Love and faithfulness will meet.
Righteousness and peace will kiss.

(Psalm 85.10)

Pause

Love your neighbour as you love yourself.

(Matthew 22.39)

Pause

God invites you to the Home of Peace.

(Quran – Jonah 10.25)

Silence

PRAYER FOR THE LIFE OF THE WORLD

To the home of peace
to the field of love
to the land where forgiveness and right relationship meet
we look, O God,
with longing for earth's children
with compassion for the creatures
with hearts breaking for the nations and people we love.
Open us to visions we have never known
strengthen us for self-givings we have never made
delight us with a oneness we could never have imagined
that we may truly be born of You
makers of peace.

Silent prayers for peace

PRAYER OF BLESSING

May the love of life
fill our hearts.
May the love of earth
bring joy to heaven.
May the love of self
deepen our souls.
May the love of neighbour
heal our world.
As nations, as peoples, as families this day
may the love of life heal our world.

SATURDAY EVENING

Blessed are the peacemakers
for they are born of God.
(Matthew 5.9)

PRAYER OF AWARENESS

It is because we long for peace
that we pray.
It is because we hope for wholeness
that we hunger.
It is because we need forgiveness
that we seek new beginnings.
So we come
entering the depths of our soul
to plead for peace
to summon wholeness
to beg forgiveness
of ourselves and one another
and thus of You
Soul within our soul
Light within our longings.

Be still and aware

SCRIPTURE AND MEDITATION

God makes wars cease to the end of the earth.

(Psalm 46.9)

Pause

Love your enemy and pray for those who harm you.

(Matthew 5.44)

Pause

God created us as one soul
and as one soul God will bring us back to life.

(Quran – Luqman 31.28)

Silence

PRAYER FOR THE LIFE OF THE WORLD

Created as one soul
made in the holy image
our deepest desires are Your desires
our first instincts are Your instincts.
Renew in us our sacred longings
revive in us our first thirsts
that wars may cease
and the human soul be one
that wars may cease
and the human soul be one.

Silent prayers for peace

PRAYER OF BLESSING

Peace be ours.
the peace of the One be ours
that we may be one and many
that we may be bound and free
that we may be prisoners to love and fly like doves.
Peace be ours
the peace of the One be ours
that we may be one and many
that we may be bound and free
that we may be prisoners to love and fly.

APPENDIX
Hebrew, Christian, and Muslim Art

The artwork used throughout this book comes from the Hebrew, Christian, and Islamic worlds of art. The *Golden Haggadah* from 14th-century Spain is one of the most beautifully illuminated manuscripts of Passover ritual in the Hebrew tradition. Similarly the *Lindisfarne Gospels* from seventh-century Britain is celebrated as among the finest expressions of illuminated gospel text in the Christian world. And equally the artistic genius of carpet design in fourteenth-century Egypt was part of what made the Mamluk capital of Cairo the artistic centre of the Arab Islamic world. The other piece of artwork used by Vera Brice, the graphics artist who has so beautifully woven together text and illumination in this prayer book, is a section of fourteenth-century mosaic from the Alhambra Palace in Granada, in which the Moorish culture of Spain blended the skills of Muslim, Jewish and Christian artists to reflect the theme of paradise on earth in the fountains, court-yards and palace of Alhambra.

Many features of this artwork could be commented on as well as the cross-fertilisation that obviously occurred over centuries and across great expanses of the then-known world as a result of east–west trade in silks and spices. But I am struck above all else by two shared themes in the artwork of this book. One is the use of circular design or mandala imagery to point to the deep human longing for wholeness. Whether it is in the matzah, the round unleavened bread of freedom depicted in the *Golden*

Haggadah, or the disk that represents creation at the heart of the Celtic cross in the *Lindisfarne Gospels,* or the sphere at the centre of the Mamluk carpet that expresses the oneness from which life in its geometric forms and proportions emerge – in all of this the circle or the mandala offers a vision of wholeness as essential to true holiness.

The other feature that consistently appears in the artwork of these three great spiritual traditions is the theme of interwovenness. This in fact is the predominant theme in the Alhambra Palace mosaic, each strand threaded under, over, and through every other strand. In the carpet page design of the *Lindisfarne Gospels,* all life forms are interrelated, the abstract shape of one creature woven inseparably through the lines of another. Similarly in the lattice-work patterns that comprise the matzah in the *Golden Haggadah,* there is a sense of every part of the design interlacing with every other part in order to lead to the centre. And in the Mamluk carpet design there is a geometry to the whole that consists of an infinite variety of interconnected forms.

If as nations and religious traditions we were to follow the wisdom of artists, if we were to remember what they seem never to forget, then we would know that the themes that underlie the human soul are deeper than the patterns that distinguish us. Then we would know that the lines that distinguish us can also be the interlacing that unites us.